D1196197

Happy Birthday to
my tea partner! xoxo
gAV
Bruxelles 2007

a passion for
tea

a passion for
tea

hattie ellis
photography by debi treloar

RYLAND
PETERS
& SMALL
LONDON NEW YORK

Designer Jo Fernandes
Senior Editor Clare Double
Picture Research Emily Westlake
Production Eleanor Cant
Art Director Anne-Marie Bulat
Publishing Director Alison Starling
Stylist Emily Chalmers
Food Stylist Fiona Smith

First published in the United Kingdom in 2006
by Ryland Peters & Small
20–21 Jockey's Fields
London WC1R 4BW
www.rylandpeters.com

10 9 8 7 6 5 4 3 2 1
Text, design and photographs
© Ryland Peters & Small 2002, 2006
A longer version of this text was previously
published in *Tea* (2002).

ISBN-10: 1-84597-227-9
ISBN-13: 978-1-84597-227-1
Printed and bound in China

contents

MAJANI
CHAI
TA
RENTA

PREMIUM
BRAND TEA

生煙
龍鳳寶氣

JASMINE TEA

CHINA FUJIAN OOLONG TEA

Oolong

what is tea?

The leaves of a plant of the *Camellia* family + hot water = tea. This simple equation sums up the most popular drink in the world. Yet this everyday drink is far from ordinary. Tea has inspired poetry and porcelain. Tea brightens mornings, refreshes afternoons and warms nights. Tea soothes frayed nerves and stimulates tired minds. Tea brings people together around food, conversation and hospitality. Tea has sent trading ships racing around the globe and intertwines with religion, medicine and art.

Gathered in from lands afar, these quiet packets in our kitchen cupboards contain a world of flavours. From India, there is the subtle fineness of a single-estate Darjeeling and the chirpy vigour of an Assam; from China, a vast range of sophisticated teas, imbued with the poetry of tastes and names such as Dragon Well and Silver Needles; or the elegant jade of Japanese green teas and the scented decorum of an Earl Grey flavoured with citrus bergamot oil.

A Passion for Tea is about how you can expand your knowledge and appreciation of tea to enjoy and explore its wide range of scents and flavours.

the tradition

the origins of tea

Around 4,700 years ago, the story goes, wild tea leaves fell into a pot of boiling water. The resulting infusion was sipped by Chinese emperor Shen Nung. 'It quenches thirst,' he noted. 'It gladdens and cheers the heart.'

Another story tells how Bodhidharma, the founder of Zen Buddhism, meditated for nine years. At one point he fell asleep and was so upset by his tiredness that he cut off his eyelids and threw them to the earth. At the spot where they fell, tea plants sprang up. From that day, the serrated ovals of tea leaves would be ever watchful against sloth.

The Chinese have woven tea into their stories, their philosophy, their art and their literature, and daily lives. Successive dynasties produced different styles of tea-drinking, and sophisticated ceramics to suit. Tea became a part of body, mind, spirit and home. This Chinese passion was given a text by the eighth-century scholar, Lu Yu, whose treatise *Classic of Tea* brought together such knowledge as how to grow the plants and the use of 20 different types of water to make the brew, along with poetic descriptions of leaves that shrink and crinkle like a Mongol's boots.

spread around the world

After being enjoyed in China, then Japan, for hundreds of years, tea reached Europe in the 17th century when Portuguese and Dutch traders brought it back as a luxury alongside silks and spices. In 1662, the Portuguese Catherine of Braganza included a chest of tea in her dowry when she married the British king, Charles II, and the drink became the height of sophistication among the aristocracy. Precious leaves were locked in caddies, and the brew was drunk from the new porcelain imported from the East. Named 'china' after its country of origin, this acted as ballast in the ships with the tea stored above. Meanwhile, caravans of camels brought tea across mountain and desert from China to Russia.

Tea drinking developed in America until the Boston Tea Party of 1773, when patriots threw chestfuls of tea into the sea in protest at British taxation. Tea was costly in Europe, because of the expense of importing it from China and because Europeans did not know the craft of tea-making. But by the second half of the 19th century, swift clipper ships raced to bring the new season's teas to the West.

In the 19th century, the British Empire helped make tea a daily drink for workers and wealthy alike, as botanists and entrepreneurs set up tea plantations in India. Because it is made with boiling water, tea is thought to have reduced urban disease – so this energizing drink helped power the Industrial Revolution.

tea in literature and art

Tea has long featured in the domestic scenes of painting and literature. Eighteenth-century portraits depict rich families gathered around a tea table, with the porcelain and tea caddies displaying their good taste.

The calm, clean energy of tea has also inspired writers. French authors of the 17th and 18th centuries, such as Racine, took to the new brew, as did the British. 'Tea! Thou soft, thou sober, sage and venerable liquid, thou female tongue-running, smile-soothing, heart-opening, wink-tippling cordial …' wrote Colley Cibber in 1708. The Romantic poets Coleridge and Byron wrote of tea, while Shelley downed cup after cup.

The Japanese haiku master, Issa, even chose to become the 'cup-of-tea' poet, symbolizing how he found the beautiful in daily life. James Joyce included the plume of steam from the kettle spout and the sham Crown Derby in the domestic details of Leopold Bloom's day in *Ulysses*, and the writings of Jane Austen, Henry James, Tolstoy, Turgenev and Thackeray all feature tea as part of ordinary life. In Lewis Carroll's *Alice's Adventures in Wonderland*, teatime is given a nonsensical twist at the Mad Hatter's tea party, whilst Proust famously uses some crumbs of madeleine soaked in tea as a conduit to *Remembrance of Things Past*.

the teas

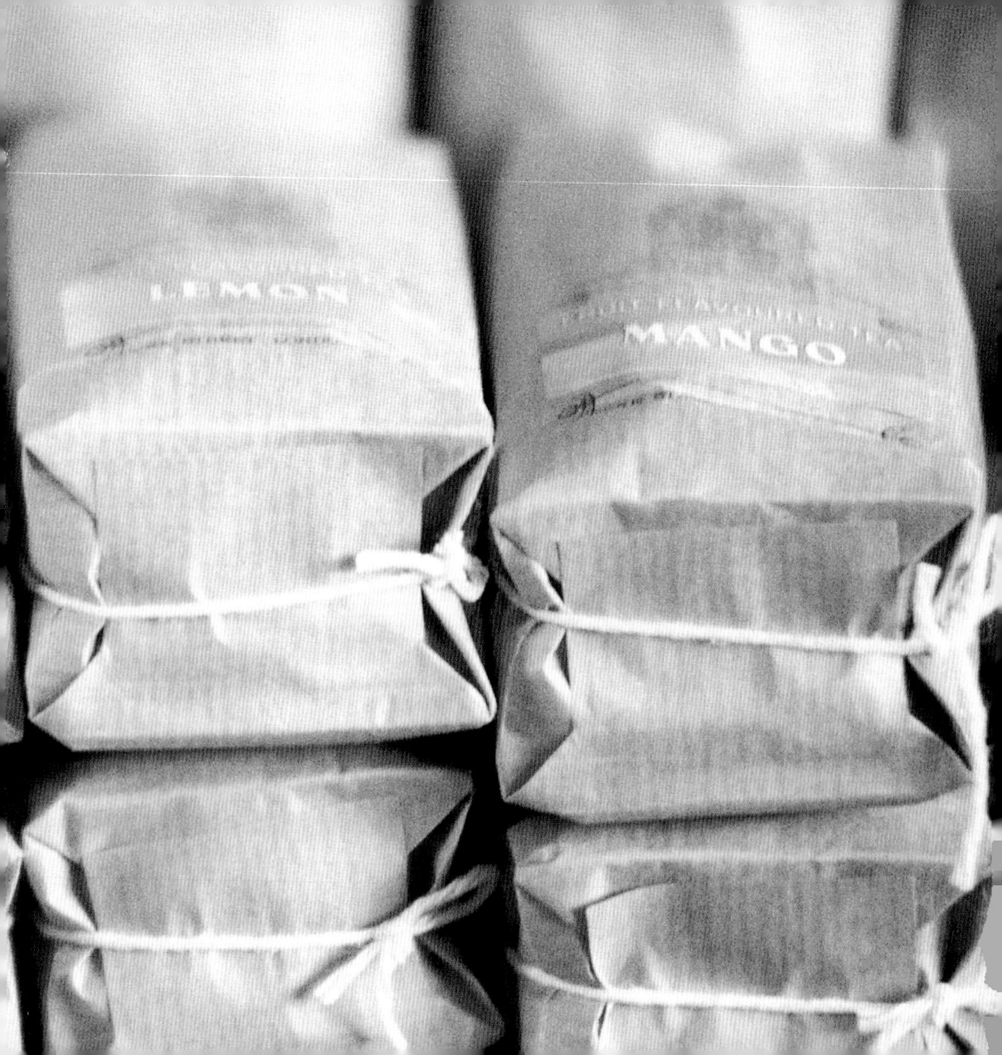
LEMON
MANGO

tea plants

High on Himalayan mountains, tucked into the plots of Chinese smallholders and in Japanese tea gardens, grows a relative of the garden camellia. There are two main varieties of tea plant; *Camellia sinensis*, which gives Chinese teas, and the Indian *Camellia assamica*.

The shiny green tea leaves are harvested regularly so the tender young tops return again and again. The top two leaves of the plant plus the closed bud, or tip, make the finest grades. Lower leaves make the coarser varieties. Tea leaves can be cut to make tannic, quick-brewing tea, or made into subtler, more distinctive leaf teas. Especially prized, in areas with a limited growing season, are the vibrant flavours of the first growth, or first flush, of leaves. High altitudes, with a shorter and slower growing season, make the flavour of such leaves even more intense, which is why some of the best teas grow on mountainsides in places such as Darjeeling, and the high slopes of China's Yunnan province.

Camellia sinensis

Opposite, top row, from left
Castleton Darjeeling (India);
Tommagong BOPF (Sri
Lanka), Gyokuro (Japan).

Middle row, from left
Fujian Phoenix Eye white tea
(China); Lapsang Souchong
Imperial black smoked tea
(China); Hyson (China).

Bottom row, from left
Chun Mee (China); Grand
Oolong (Taiwan); Gunpowder
Zhy Cha green tea (China).

black, green, oolong and white tea

All teas start from green leaves. It is processing that determines whether they are black, green or oolong. To make black tea, plucked tea leaves are first withered to make them more pliable. The partially dried leaves are then rolled to release their juices and enzymes. There follows a process of oxidation, which produces the characteristic flavour and colour of black tea. Finally, the tea is fired with hot air to destroy enzymes and stabilize the leaves.

Green tea, by contrast, is made from unoxidized leaves, which are simply heated to destroy the enzymes that would cause oxidation. They are then rolled to release their flavours, and finally dried to stabilize the tea. Green tea leaves contain the sweetness and many of the vitamins and other beneficial properties of the fresh green leaf, making it both healthy and a fragrant, delicious drink.

Oolong teas are a cross between black and green, with the oxidation stopped after a short time. They retain the freshness of green teas while taking on the subtle flavours and maturity of black.

Rare and precious, white teas are a Chinese speciality. The leaf-tips are hand-picked while still in bud and then dried. White tea is a pale, delicately fragrant infusion that is offered to honoured guests. It is like sipping serenity.

The Indians, Sri Lankans and Africans are best known for their black teas; the Japanese specialize in green teas, and the Chinese make all four kinds.

India and Sri Lanka

Darjeeling – known as the 'tea of mountain mists' – grows high on the foothills of the Himalayan range. The height and coolness are crucial to this Champagne of teas. Slow growth produces leaves of a delicate power with hints of Muscat grapes, perfumed roses and citrus fruits. A fine, white cup of pale gold Darjeeling, drunk without milk, is the captivating queen of drinks.

Some Darjeelings are labelled with the name of the tea garden, such as Castleton, Tukdah, Margaret's Hope and Badamtam. These places, through the soil and the specific growing conditions, give fascinating variations in taste in the same way that different vineyards give character to wine. First-flush teas, sought out by tea lovers, are the lightest and most refreshingly aromatic.

Assam teas, grown in the north-east of India, come from the native Indian tea plant, whose leaves are slightly less sweet than the Chinese plant. The teas are invigorating, malty, strong, full-bodied and sometimes almost spicy. The highlands of southern India, such as the Nilgiris, are also famed for their fine, fragrantly fruity teas, some of which are comparable in style to Ceylon teas.

The best teas from Sri Lanka, still marketed under the island's former name of Ceylon, are also high-grown and include those from the highest tea-producing region on the island, Nuwara Eliya. Each of the six regions – Dimbula, Nuwara Eliya, Uva, Kandy, Galle and Ratnapura – produces tea of a different character, due to their individual climates and growing conditions.

China

'All the tea in China' encompasses an astonishing range. The longevity of the Chinese tea-drinking habit has resulted in thousands of categories of teas, some still handmade using ancient skills.

Chinese green teas are shaped into distinctive forms, such as pellets of Gunpowder tea, which rattle into the teapot like shot, or elegantly arched Chun Mee (Precious Eyebrow tea). Some prized teas are grown amid fruit blossom or mountain orchids. The best jasmine tea is made by putting closed flowers into tea boxes overnight, when they will open and impart their heady scent to the tea leaves. The process is repeated several times.

Chinese black teas are often softly fragrant and refreshing, such as the rolled Keemuns with their red-brown liquor, and teas from the provinces of Yunnan and Szechuan, with hints of almonds, flowers and spices. They were traditionally transported as bricks (above), which today are just enjoyed for their decorative value. Tarry, black Lapsang Souchong is a smoked tea made by withering and drying the leaves over pine fires.

Oolong teas are some of China's most sophisticated teas. Look out, also, for the rare white teas, such as Silver Needles.

Japan

Japanese tea is the white wine of brews – a fine, fragrant, pale drink that shines with a greeny-gold light. In a country with such a sophisticated visual sense and palate, colour and delicacy of taste are important.

The finest Japanese tea, Gyokuro (Precious Dewdrop), makes production an art form, with bushes shaded so the leaves produce extra chlorophyll, resulting in a beautiful jade tea with a fresh, herbaceous taste that is smoothly fragrant and sweet. The renowned powdered tea, Matcha, is made from Gyokuro, and this is whisked into an astringent frothy green tea to be drunk in the famous Japanese tea ceremony.

Sencha is the high-quality grade of Japanese green tea and can be labelled with the place of origin. The leaves are carefully harvested and steamed after picking so they retain a deep green colour that is accompanied by an appealing freshness of taste. The grassy-tasting early teas of the season are much prized and given as presents.

Bancha is an everyday drink that can be made from leaves harvested when the tea bushes are shaped; Kukicha uses large leaves and stems. Genmaicha includes puffed rice, which mellows green tea. Hojicha is a roasted tea whose smoky, savoury strength is good with Japanese food.

Taiwan

Taiwan is famous for its oolong teas, known as Formosa oolongs from the island's former name. 'Oolong' means 'black dragon', after the story of a planter who, following his nose to a delicious fragrance, found a tea bush with the lucky omen of a serpent curled around it. He made tea with the leaves and was captivated by their sensual scent. Being semi-oxidized teas, oolongs are defined by the method of production rather than a particular plant. However, like the leaves in the story, they delight drinkers with their floral notes, hints of fruity fragrance and peach-like beauty. The teas range from lightly oxidized oolongs, such as Jade Oolong and Pouchong, through to dark oolongs such as White Tip or Oriental Beauty. Some of the most famous, such as Tung Ting, come from mountainous central Taiwan.

tea blends

Dedicated tea merchants create and maintain house blends, tasting and mixing teas that will vary according to where they come from and even the day of harvest, to ensure that they have a consistent character.

English Breakfast tea might include malty Assams and full-flavoured Ceylon and African teas in a blend designed to stand up to a hearty breakfast. Irish Breakfast blends suit the traditional national taste for a strong, dark, punchy brew. Afternoon Tea blends are lighter, perhaps mixing Darjeelings with aromatic black Chinese teas.

An aristocratic classic, Earl Grey is flavoured with the oil of the citrus bergamot fruit. Russian Caravan teas imitate the taste of the smoky teas carried on the long trek from China. Floral teas such as rose, jasmine and violet use dried petals to make delicate, fragrant cupfuls. Other flavoured teas might include such ingredients as dried citrus peel and spices.

It is easy to create your own blends at home, perhaps using a black tea as a base for colour and body, enlivened with a fragrant oolong, a Darjeeling or a smoky souchong, or with the addition of flowers, citrus peel or dried fruits for a modern flavoured blend.

infusions

For centuries, other plants have also been infused
in hot water and drunk for their restorative
qualities. Chamomile, famous as a relaxing
infusion, was used in Roman times to ease period
pains. Crushed fennel seeds ease wind in children
and adults. Ginger is an ancient remedy for colds.
Russian cosmonauts took ginseng to protect them
from infection when confined in space, and others
use it to increase their energy. Aromatic hops
promote sleep, while lavender is used for tension
and halitosis. Rosemary has potent, aromatic oils
for concentration and energy, and acts as an
antioxidant. Thyme helps with headaches and is an
antiseptic. Vervain is prized by the French for liver
problems, and aids the digestion. Refreshing mint
is a digestive that soothes you into a sweet night's
sleep and scented lemon verbena, taken for nerves
and indigestion, is also drunk for its great taste.

the tasting

buying and storing

Specialist tea retailers offer a wide range, including their own blends, and can advise you on what to explore. Tea keeps well, so it is worth stocking up at a good tea merchant or specialist website every so often.

Store tea away from sunlight and heat in airtight caddies. If you leave it in the packet, clip the top to keep air out. To enjoy the freshest tastes, use green tea within six months and black tea within a year. Tea keeps best in larger quantities, which is why specialist shops have big containers from which they weigh out the leaves for each purchase.

When buying Indian and Ceylon teas, 'FOP' means Flowery Orange Pekoe (pronounced 'peck-oh'), referring to the delicate bud and top leaf at the end of each shoot. This indicates a high grade of tea. Grading can go all the way up to 'SFTGFOP' – Special Finest Tippy Golden Flowery Orange Pekoe – quite literally a tip-top tea. 'Orange Pekoe' means the next leaf down from the top leaf and is also a good grade of tea. Broken teas of all grades have a 'B' in their label and make stronger, darker brews suitable for a more bracing breakfast drink.

equipment

China is a very good material for teapots and cups because it retains the heat of the brew and does not alter its flavour. Glass pots are a modern alternative and let you see the whole leaf tea unfurl as the tea brews. Look for a pot with a handle you can hold easily without burning your fingers and with a lid that will stay on when pouring. The first teapots in the world were made in Yixing in China, at a time when tea-making evolved from whipping powdered tea to infusing whole leaves in water. These beautiful pots of unglazed stoneware are still made today, and, over time, the porous material becomes infused with the flavour of the tea.

A plain white china cup is best for showing off the colours that distinguish different teas. To brew a single mug of loose-leaf tea you can also use an infuser mug with a removable mesh basket, or an infuser ball.

Teapots are now available with infuser baskets for the leaves, which you can remove after the tea has been brewed for the right length of time to prevent it stewing. You can also brew the tea Chinese-style in a tea bowl, refreshing the leaves with new water for successive brews.

making the perfect cup

How you brew your tea is down to personal taste and the specific leaves and brewing vessel you are using, so experiment with the following guidelines to find out what works best for you.

• For black and oolong teas, you need about one rounded teaspoon of whole leaves per cup; slightly less for broken, unless you like strong tea. For green tea and fine white teas, use two rounded teaspoons per cup.

• Use freshly drawn, cold water and bring to the boil. Turn off the kettle immediately the water boils or it becomes de-oxygenated and the resulting brew will be less bright in flavour.

• Warm the pot – or cup, if using an infuser – by swilling hot water around the inside, then pouring it away.

• Pour just-boiled water onto black and oolong teas, but for green and white teas leave the water to cool a little (70–80°C, and around 50°C for Gyokuro) before pouring onto the leaves. Leave the boiled water in the kettle for two to three minutes to get it to around 80°C.

• Black tea needs about five minutes' brewing for whole leaves, two to three for broken. Fine Darjeelings and green tea need two or three minutes. Oolongs need about seven minutes, white about ten. Tea left on the leaves too long, especially green tea, becomes astringent and bitter.

adding milk, citrus and sugar

Which comes first, tea or milk? This question continues to rattle tea tables. Some say milk was put in first to protect the precious china of early teacups from hot tea. It mixes better with the tea and stops the fats developing a 'cooked' taste. Others believe that adding milk to tea helps you to judge the right amount to put in.

Brisk, strong black teas such as Assam and English Breakfast blends are designed for the Western habit of adding milk. Milk can muffle the delicate flavours of a tea such as a first-flush Darjeeling. It is unsuitable for the subtle freshness of green and oolong teas, and inconceivable with ultra-fine white teas.

Russians may take a spoonful of jam in tea. It is a custom there and in the Middle East to drink tea through a sugar lump held between the teeth or dissolving in the mouth. Sugar takes the edge off subtle teas, but a spoonful of sugar or honey can bring out the flavour of herbal infusions such as North African mint tea.

Some people add a lemon slice to black tea instead of milk; first-flush Darjeelings taste remarkably lemony without this addition. As a change, try a slice of orange in an aromatic tea such as Earl Grey.

tea and food

Teas and foods have evolved to suit each other. Dim sum developed in Canton teahouses as snacks to eat with tea. The British like strong teas with fried breakfasts and fish and chips, and Darjeeling with sandwiches for afternoon tea. Savoury Japanese green teas are perfectly suited to drinking with sushi and sashimi. The ever-ready samovar meant tea could sustain Russians before and after their main meal.

As an ingredient in food, tea is valued for its flavour and colour. The Chinese crack the shells of hard-boiled eggs and simmer them in tea and soy sauce to marble the whites with dark veins. For a famous Szechuan dish, duck is smoked in a wok over tea, sugar and rice. The Japanese use bright green powdered tea to make green-tea ice cream; the Burmese eat tea pickled, in a dish called *lepet*, to revive them after meals.

Tea adds fragrance to sweet dishes. Home bakers soak dried vine fruits in it to make teabreads; fusion chefs coat exotic fruits in spiced tea syrups, and French chocolatiers use such flavours as Earl Grey and jasmine in ganaches.

tea and health

Tea was first consumed for its beneficial properties, which science has since proved. As well as containing minerals and vitamins, tea has a good dose of polyphenols, which act as antioxidants mopping up free radicals that damage the body. These polyphenols are particularly potent in green tea, which is why it is promoted as a healthy drink. Tea is also thought to act against such problems as heart disease, cancer and tooth decay.

Tea contains less caffeine per cup than coffee, but if you want to lessen the caffeine content of your tea, infuse as briefly as possible or drink green tea (apart from Japanese Matcha, which has a buzz).

chai masala

100 ml milk

2 teaspoons sugar

1 teaspoon black tea

¼ teaspoon freshly ground nutmeg

¼ teaspoon finely grated fresh ginger
or a pinch of ground ginger

3 cloves

seeds of 3 green cardamom pods

a pinch of ground cinnamon

makes 2 small cups

This spiced Indian tea can be used to ward off and relieve colds, but
has become popular in the West as a delicious drink in its own right.

Put 200 ml water with the milk and sugar in a saucepan. Add the tea and
spices. Bring to the boil, reduce the heat and simmer for 2 minutes.
Strain into cups and serve.

Try altering the spice mixture to suit your own taste. Use ground ginger
if making a larger quantity, and mix the spices well before use.

Japanese tea ceremony

This ceremony or 'way of tea' consists of the making, serving and drinking of tea. Guests enter the teahouse through a garden, first rinsing their hands and mouth as a gesture of purification. They are served food of seasonal ingredients, colours and shapes, and two kinds of tea by a tea practitioner.

The tea served is Matcha, finest powdered green tea. It is mixed with hot water in the tea bowl using a small whisk of split bamboo. The first brew is thick and the guests drink a few sips in turn from a shared vessel. The principal guest asks the name of the tea, and the utensils and bowl are appreciated by the participants. Little sweets are made to be eaten with the tea. A second, thinner tea is served in individual bowls, whisked to have a frothy top.

Every detail builds into the meaning of the event. The ritual embodies the respect, sharing and consideration at the heart of hospitality.

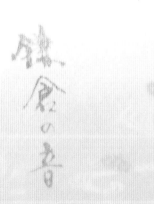

English afternoon tea

Forty per cent of every drop drunk in the UK still comes in the form of 'a cuppa' – a total of 165 million cups a day. The great comforter, reviver and warmer of the British soul, tea even has its own mealtime in the form of afternoon tea. This institution gained popularity in the 19th century as dinner was served later, leaving a hungry gap as the clock struck five.

The meal has inspired its own edibles. Sandwiches can be savoury (such as cucumber or watercress) or sweet, with jam or honey. The cakes might include a light sponge, a dark fruitcake or a rich chocolate cake. Perhaps the tea table might be spread with crumpets dripping with butter, scones with clotted cream and strawberry jam. Ham and eggs and other savoury foods may be served for the more substantial 'high tea', which replaces an evening meal altogether.

The teapot crowns the regal tea service, displayed on a white tablecloth in the drawing room or on a garden table in summertime. But afternoon tea is still taken even if it is just a mugful and a biscuit in front of the office computer.

Earl Grey punch

2 tablespoons Earl Grey tea

freshly squeezed juice of 1 lemon

300 ml orange juice

150 ml apple juice

220 ml ginger ale

1 tablespoon caster sugar

2 sprigs of mint

10 ice cubes

dark rum, to taste (optional)

Makes about 1 litre

The tea in this fruit punch stops it being too sweet and makes it a more refreshing drink. The punch also adds a fragrant edge to fruit salad.

Put the tea into a teapot. Measure 300 ml boiling water and pour it over the tea. Set aside to infuse for 4 minutes. Meanwhile, pour the fruit juices, ginger ale and sugar into a jug. Add the infused tea and stir to dissolve all the sugar. Add the mint.

Let cool, then chill in the refrigerator. Remove the mint and serve in the jug with ice cubes added.

Alternatively fill 4 glasses with ice cubes and pour over the punch. If using rum, stir into the punch before adding the ice.

tea in America

The tea-drinking habit was probably brought to the eastern coast of the United States by Dutch settlers. Tea pleasure gardens sprang up, where people could meet, drink, see and be seen. After the Boston Tea Party US patriots shunned tea in favour of other infusions. Coffee has become more of a national drink, but tea is still popular in the States, and no less a person than George Washington was an avid imbiber.

The tea bag was created by New York tea merchant, Thomas Sullivan. He sent out single samples of tea in little silk bags and was astonished when customers asked for supplies not just of the tea but of the bags too.

In recent years there has been a surge of interest in leaf teas in the US. Specialist traders offer the likes of estate Darjeelings, fragrant oolongs, green teas and own-label blends.

American iced tea

Iced tea was first presented to Americans at the St Louis World Fair in 1904.

The basic principle is to make strong tea – twice as much tea as you would normally use – and pour it over ice cubes (about 3–4 per glass) into a ceramic jug. To this you can add any number of ingredients to taste, such as freshly squeezed orange, lemon or lime juice and sugar, again to taste. Alternatively, add herbs or spices such as mint or finely grated ginger root. Iced green tea is refreshingly delicious, too, and you can experiment with fragrant floral blends.

Iced tea can also be made by putting tea in water and leaving it out in the sun. For clear, rather than cloudy, iced tea infuse the leaves in cold water overnight in the refrigerator.

North African mint tea

2 teaspoons Chinese green tea,
such as gunpowder

1 sprig of mint (spearmint is
authentic, but other mints will do)

¼–1 teaspoon caster sugar, to taste

serves 1

The North African way is to pour this tea from a great height, creating
bubbles on the surface of the drink. Mint tea is traditionally drunk in
small, often decorative, glasses that are frequently replenished, and can
be accompanied by delicious, sticky-sweet pastries.

Put the green tea and mint into a teapot. Pour 250 ml just-off-the-boil
water into the pot and leave to infuse for 3 minutes. Strain the mint tea
into a glass or cup. Stir in sugar, to taste. Some people like to put pine
nuts into the glass: they soften as they soak and are eaten at the end.

useful addresses

Algerian Coffee Stores
52 Old Compton Street
London W1D 4PB
020 7437 2480
www.algcoffee.co.uk

Aroma Tea and Coffee Merchants
8a St Marys Place
Shrewsbury SY1 1DZ
01743 367598
www.aroma-coffee.co.uk

Better Beverage Company
204 Morrison Street
Edinburgh EH3 8EA
0131 4762600
www.betterbeverage.co.uk

Bettys and Taylors by Post
Pagoda House
Plumpton Park
Harrogate HG2 7LD
0845 3453636
www.bettysbypost.com

Bodum
24 Neal Street
London WC2 9QW
020 7240 9176
www.bodum.com

The Bramah Tea and Coffee Museum
40 Southwark Street
London SE1 1UN
020 7403 5650
www.bramahmuseum.co.uk

Drury Tea & Coffee Co.
3 New Row
London WC2N 4LH
020 7836 1960
www.drury.uk.com

East Teas
Borough Market
8 Southwark Street
London SE1 1TL
020 7394 0226
www.eastteas.com

Farrers
13 Stricklandgate
Kendal LA9 4LY
01539 731707
www.farrers.com

Fortnum and Mason
181 Piccadilly
London W1A 1ER
020 7734 8040
www.fortnumandmason.co.uk

Gillards of Bath
55 Guildhall Market
Bath BA2 4AW
01225 311888
www.gillards.co.uk

H. R. Higgins (Coffee-Man) Ltd
79 Duke Street
London W1K 5AS
020 7629 3913
www.hrhiggins.co.uk

Imperial Teas and Coffees
26 Steep Hill
Lincoln LN2 1LU
01522 560008
www.imperialteas.co.uk

Japan Centre Food Shop
212 Piccadilly
London W1J 9HG
020 7434 4218
www.japancentre.com

Layton Fern & Co. Ltd
27 Rathbone Place
London W1T 1EP
020 7636 2237
www.laytonfern.fsnet.co.uk
Superlative teas and coffees since 1893. Wholesale and direct mail.

Markus Coffee Company
13 Connaught Street
London W2 2AY
020 7723 4020

Mecca Tea and Coffee Merchants
25 Chalybeate Street
Aberystwyth SY23 1HX
01970 612888

Pumphrey's of Newcastle
Bridge Street, Blaydon
Tyne & Wear NE21 4JH
0191 4144510
www.pumphreys-coffee.co.uk

Selfridges
400 Oxford Street
London W1A 1AB
08708 377377
www.selfridges.com

The Tea House
15a Neal Street
London WC2H 9PU
020 7240 7539

Whittard of Chelsea
T-Zone
38 Covent Garden Market
London WC2E 8RF
020 7379 6599
www.whittard.co.uk

Wilkinson's of Norwich
5 Lobster Lane
Norwich NR2 1DQ
01603 625121
www.wilkinsonsofnorwich.com

Thanks to the following companies for loan of props for photography.

After Noah
121 Upper Street
London N1 1QP
020 7359 4281
www.afternoah.com
Eclectic homewares.

Nicole Farhi Home
17 Clifford Street
London W1X 8BY
020 7494 9051
www.nicolefarhi.com
Carefully chosen collection of old and new homewares.

Adamczewski
196 High Street
Lewes BN7 2NS
01273 470105
www.finehouseware.co.uk
Fine housewares and Yixing stoneware teapots and caddies.

David Mellor
4 Sloane Square
London SW1W 8EE
020 7730 4259
www.davidmellordesign.co.uk
Specialists in award-winning cutlery and fine kitchenware.

Minamoto Kitchoan
44 Piccadilly
London W1J 0DS
020 7437 3135
www.kitchoan.com
Beautiful Japanese sweets for the traditional tea ceremony.

Helena Rohner
c/Almendro 4
Madrid 28005, Spain
00 34 91 36 57 906
Handcrafted tableware in ceramic and wood.

To Gordon Smith

picture credits

All photographs by Debi Treloar except the following:

Philip Webb
Pages 23 below, 32 below right, 43, 45, 53, 56

Peter Cassidy
Pages 32 below left, 46, 60

William Lingwood
Endpapers, pages 33, 59

James Merrell
Page 48, 55

David Montgomery
Pages 3, 23 above

Caroline Arber
Page 32 above right

David Loftus
Page 11 left

Polly Wreford
Pages 4–5

Francesca Yorke
Page 47

PUBLISHER'S ACKNOWLEDGMENTS
The publisher would like to thank H. R. Higgins
(Coffee-Man) Ltd and Layton Fern & Co. Ltd
for allowing us to photograph in their premises.